I0569458

dear my love,

ariel west jr

to my mourning dove
of a beautiful dawn,
my love song to you.

contents

"talking"

march 8, 2023

i fell impulsively in love with her,
without thought but without regret.
my divine attention was hers.
the word choice, her voice, her entire sound
gave birth to stars in my eyes.
at any given look she could tell that i was hers,
especially when she talked about the constellations.
not the ones in the sky but the ones in my eye,
it truly astonished me
and it was all because she spoke in poetry.

this was the first poem i ever wrote about you
and it was also the same day we first met

i like

i like your smile
and i also like your voice
which i've said many times before.
i like your lips and your laugh.
oh your laugh is so cute,
i like how you love to sing
but you're still kind of shy.
i like your gentleness
and how you're kind and caring,
i like that God made you this way.
i like that i think about you all the time,
i like how i still have the image of how beautiful
you looked in the dimmed light of your room
when we watched vanilla sky.
i found out all of this information about you
within the tiny screen on my phone,
and even though i have never seen
or heard these things in the physical with my eyes,
i still like it.

incoming love

i slowly feel you becoming the words to my poetry,
oh how i love this excitement.
my hands write in motions in which cursive
gets jealous of,
and you make it easy to imagine singing these words.
my voice is not at all like yours,
not as pleasant and angelic
but you turn my words powerful
and i become able to force relentless transcribes.
in my finite life i race to jot down every breathtaking
move you make,
i slowly feel you moving my heart towards you.
i worry my books will only consist of poems about you
and nothing else,
but truthfully
if love comes from whatever you are doing to me
then i have never been this happy
to be fearful in my life.
i am dangerously fond of you,
oddly content with your natural radiance
and persuasive beauty.
i am not a fool,
but both love and incoming love will always be
my heart's basis and strongest pursuit.

cellphone

regular texts
emojis and risky flirts
fast heart rates
and anticipating replies.
this remained the same
in addition to something that came naturally,
almost unnoticed.
it became a norm for us
before you were even mine
before i was yours,
i guess it was inevitable.
you said it first,
and i didn't hesitate to use it after
but we embraced this word.
it was special and heartwarming
it was better than flirting
it didn't overwhelm the pace that we were moving
it was natural
and it was "baby."

a little transaction

a thrill came with the excitement i had
when i would surprise you with a poem.
i loved showing you my new works,
and you always loved them too.
i loved this little transaction between us,
i loved it so much.

dawn of our relation

i almost got carried away while speaking to you,
i almost said, "when i talk to you it feels right."
and at that moment it felt too soon to speak like this,
so instead i just said that it feels good.
but if you're reading this now just know that
it felt so right when you and i merged voices
into a conversation.
from the very early beginning,
from the dawn of our relation
it felt so undeniably right to me.

one more day

i like you so much i feel like it's just gonna take
one more day until i fall in love.

a good thing

why am i so compelled to write down this feeling,
i have not seen your face in person
nor heard the sound of your voice that is not
through an electronic device
but inside lies a feeling that deeply believes in you.
my passionate belief that you are the one,
the one who i will protect under the Lord's
commitment, and my own personal commandment.
right now, i am either a fool
or a prophetic lover inscribing our unity before it
seems possible.
and as i read the book of psalm
my mind flew to you and recognized days
that have not been lived through yet.
i couldn't ignore this bizarre feeling
that i knew who you were going to be to me.

a good thing pt. two

white clothing
and golden spirits in the air of the affair,
angels overhead and love underneath.
this vision starts the beginning of a forever story
powered by the moon of the night,
the laughter of our souls take a well earned pleasure
while the King stands proud of His servants.
i see precious metal,
and rocks from the ground's core.
i see a kiss that is the first of its kind.

waiting for you

more than 3 months before
i'm already planning and buying the things i need
to make our dates as special as i can.
my excitement makes it hard to not buy things that
spoil long before you come,
like the strawberries and flowers i need for our
picnic.
it's like i'm gathering everything i need,
everything i want to somehow satisfy my
eagerness;
all in efforts of trying to make this wait of the only
thing i want but can't have–
more tolerable.

love is without time

if we let love lead the way instead of ourselves
we would be lost in a field of sweetness
and stranded in the oceans of each other.
if we let love lead the way
you would already be mine,
but we play this unspoken game
of keeping this thing hidden.
if we would just forget the minds inside our heads,
love would be forced into exposure
and would consume our connection.
but again, we play this game in fear of it being too
soon.
baby girl, with love,
time doesn't exist
and no boundary bounds its reach.

trying patience

i want you but can't tell you yet
and the fact that you don't know
puts my chances at zero,
and living while knowing
there's no possibility makes it so difficult
to be patient.
but when i write it down,
i feel as if i'm pouring out these feelings
and i feel just a little more comfortable with waiting.

the first ones

people have fallen in love before,
but they haven't felt quite like this.
it feels like we are the first ones
to fall in whatever this is.

the truth

i felt so comfortable reading my poems to you
but whenever i said the word "love,"
i told you that was just me bringing the poem to its full
potential, to make it more meaningful,
but really that word was meant for you.
you being my inspiration was my disclaimer from
telling the truth.
we were still fairly new to each other,
but not in *my* heart.
and if i'm being honest, though i used "love"
for the benefit of the poems,
my soul knew that word was more
than just for the art of poetry,
but for the truth of how i felt for you.

sooner

i love you and it's strange because of this distance,
your soul is who i know dearly.
i talk to it everyday and we are in love.
you don't know about us yet
but your soul is my heart's mate.
my spirit has beaten me to this confession
for my flesh is delayed by the atlantic ocean
and thousands of miles of land.
my soul has fallen for yours
and they whisper songs to each other.
you may not understand if i told you now,
but these feelings are true and real and they do not
disappear merely because the physical of us
is slow to discover and slow to speak the truth.
though if this distance weren't in the way
you would of already known this feeling
and already felt my touch,
maybe you would of already felt the same,
and maybe we could of been crazy in love
a whole lot sooner.

beauty

ordinary day

i think the most beautiful thing God created
were women.
more than a sunset
or clear views of a vast mountain range,
out of every wonderful thing He made
your entirety is by far the most alluring.
there is simply nothing i could honestly say
that i would rather see
than just an ordinary day
with you right in front of me.

separate

your smile is heavenly.
i know God crafted you separate
from everyone else.

a little bit of you

the early morning resists to appear heavenly
until you grant it so,
the sky dares not to use your name in vain
as it mimics to equal the delight you have in my eyes.
therefore every time the sunrise touches the clouds
i know it is you that its beauty comes from.
you show the world how real gorgeousness should be
like, the earth watches and listens.
if you don't believe me
then wait until the next butterfly lands on a flower,
or for a rainbow to appear after a light shower,
just wait until a hill of wildflowers dance from the
wind between its leaves and stems,
or the life of water, its oceans and streams that form
pictures of art in its salty waves,
just wait until the laughter in a voice bursts of
happiness
or the cry of heartwarming joy in a moment of love,
just wait and watch and you will see a little bit of you
in every beautiful thing.
you will even find a little bit of you
in every part of my beautiful heart.

ounce

you are the same inside and out,
there is not a single ounce of you
that i don't find ravishing.

a poet's muse

in this moment i am selfish and greedy
i want a muse to love with enough strength
that i have scrolls of genuine words to say.
this creation of art in a body of flesh,
this gaze that weakens envy and hate,
it leaves a love so delicately placed
and flows effortlessly from the middle of my soul.
in the grasp of my hands
let me paint you with my words.

dear my love,

eve's daughter

what's crazy is that women are so perfectly created
by God that even some of the angels left heaven
to be amongst God's most beautiful creation.
how valuable then must you feel to hold the exact
same genetic material
that made heavenly angels fall down to earth
just for a simple experience with you?
how much more beautiful do you think you can
possibly become if you are already a woman?

those sons of God chose to leave the ultimate paradise
for just a few moments with a human woman,
a daughter of eve.
from an angel to a demon,
it is specifically my own decisions against God
that can destroy me.
so therefore, over you my darling i will not lust,
but take into account the unmeasurable power you
hold in being the most precious and prettiest thing
to have ever graced both heaven and earth.

all along

i spoke to the stars about how i have found some of
them on land,
that i have been face to face with their kind.
they laughed for they knew that stars only
belonged to the sky,
but i began to explain what i discovered.
their faces were puzzled and in shock,
they didn't understand how i could of seen
them on earth,
but they believed every word.
they recognized my illustrations and how detailed
my description was.
they told me no human without actually seeing
a star up close could have ever given a description
like that.
i had convinced them of the truth of my sight.
they were thrilled but still wanted proof,
they asked me to bring the stars i had seen,
the ones that were not beside the moon with them.
i then went and brought you to this spot
underneath the night sky,
and they found it fascinating to see that the stars
that roamed on land were all along in your eyes.

your smile

i could totally see myself
pouring my life out to you,
a weary voice
intimate and soft spoken.
i can see my tongue giving awe to itself
for having created words that get to be heard
by your ear.
if by my voice a smile forms upon your face
i will have then lost the ability of speech.
my very mouth producing words
that you take as joy would elate me,
and i may not have the strength
to see such a miracle a second time.

hair

the soft strands and your brown curls
i imagine roll over in tides,
i bet the wind thinks it tastes sweet
to run through your compelling chaos of twists
and turns.
i am in love with the beauty God blessed you with.

beauty

you are more beautiful than the birds singing in the
morning.
i woke to the movement of you over the phone
for my peace got disturbed by the uncertainty of
your well being.
my love i wanted to hear that you were okay,
that you were comfortable in bed
safe inside the house,
safe in this world of wonder that is not beautiful
enough to hold a precious you.
your surroundings lack beauty among your steps,
the ground i fear has no strength for the weight
of your delicate and delightful soul.
there is no existence of prettiness and charm
greater than you.
baby, you are more beautiful than love itself,
and because of this,
what does it mean of my love compared to
everyone else?
if my love travels to you who is more beautiful than
love itself, wouldn't that mean how i feel for you
is also the prettiest thing to ever be?
is this why my love longs to accompany your life?
my delicate flower, you are beautiful and it must be
difficult living with no reference of beauty
to look up to.
my darling, you should just look into the mirror,
for the highest standard is you.

before i met you

i think too much about who you are,
what you will look like
and how it would be,
why do i do this?
i will never come up
with the correct imagination of you.

the truth is
i wrote that first part before i met you
and dang,
i didn't know you would look this good.

my art

i begin to write a sentence with no exact end,
then i think of you
and my fingers start to tell stories.
it is quite easy to pick a wonder about you.
it excites me to scavenge your many beauties
and it challenges my competitive nature
to find correct words that match such an angel.
you are an art whose details show constant marvel,
every ounce of your breath i can use to write
amazing dreams that only you have the power
of creating.

evolutionary gaze

my eyes have never met ones that look like yours,
not because yours are the perfect palette of colors,
not because your iris has more planets in the
galaxies
and more suns then there are stars.
yours are different because you looked at me
infinitely.
you saw me the same in the past and future,
you saw me as a trying being in all circumstances.
i know because i read the words,
the craters of light spelled out in your eyes.
it said we met at the perfect time
in which nothing could separate
this evolutionary gaze.

dear my love,

a beautiful human being

she is a gentle boat in the sunrise
an island paradise
she is the dance of plants
and the way of song
a morning bird
and a graceful swan
she is a city at night
with stars on the ground instead of the sky
she is an open window
with a cool breeze
she is a hand stretched out
towards a land that i dream,
a flower born from heaven
she is a beautiful human being.

first impression

i hope you don't take this the wrong way but,
the first day i ever seen you
was also the most beautiful i have ever seen you.
i guess you can say i was marveled
and became frozen,
totally paralyzed in my favor of your beauty.

dear my love,

_____

_____

_____

_____

_____

_____

_____

_____

_____

_____

_____

_____

fond of you

in space you are more important than gravity,
the alphabet exists for your name
and the birds sing for your ears.
i admire you deeply,
beauty is enamored of you
and gets its meaning from your exceptional vibrancy.
i am fond of you,
sincerely, unapologetically, beyond in love with you.

Christ-Centered

dear my love,

gratitude

thank you God for waking me up
and giving me another day with a beautiful dawn.

God's decision

a strong God fearing woman attracts
and intimidates me at the same time.
ultimately, those are both the very reasons
i am automatically driven to dive into her character.
it's admiration that i feel,
the inspiration of her faith that moves me
to want to be like her.
after all, that's what she should be doing,
being an example of God's own image
and inspiring others to follow.
between her radiantly shining faith
and her beauty that i try to ignore,
should my pursuit of her go any further
than to follow her example of faith?
i'll let God decide that.

caught

we were caught in God's mysterious ways,
oh how lucky are we to have been stuck in this
glorious uncertainty?
i have discovered that our Father delights in His own
generosity.
oh how much luckier have i become to be caught
in this suspenseful miracle with you?
for He works His wonders in the uncertainty of things.

unconditionally trying

i have long dark hair and skin not as dark,
you love me so much for which i am eternally grateful
but my curiosity wakes me with a question i wonder.
what if i had red hair with a different shade of skin,
would the feelings you have for me change in any
measurement?
the answer to this question brings another
because depending on what you say
i wonder if what we have is unconditional
or just partly genuine?
or perhaps it is not fair to expect unconditional love
when humanity is not as perfect as God,
and although i am not perfect
i can still try to be like Him as much as possible.

hopefully you feel the same

my plan for you

God says we're supposed to submit ourselves to each other, and if you ever become mine that's what i plan to do. you're gonna laugh with me and be silly and not feel embarrassed about it. you're gonna feel so free and comfortable that you might forget your intention to always look pretty in front of me, but the good news is that you're still beautiful even when you forget. i'll be proud of everything you accomplish no matter how big or small. the point i'm trying to make is that i'm going to be entirely and only yours, so i plan to let you indulge in everything that i have to offer as a lover.

opposing feeling

this just doesn't feel real
this thing between you and i,
it still runs like a dream replaying across my mind.
my heart can't read fast enough these things
that i feel.
how can it be that you love me for me?
this is what i have been begging for, but all this time
i figured i was just praying without a genuine belief
that it could actually happen?
i thought i was just praying kind of redundantly.

my glorious God forgive me,
i know my prayers have power behind Jesus' name
but i thought this feeling was out of the question for me.
i didn't think love could be like i thought it could be,
and still, why does it feel unreal?
my mind had convinced me that the world won,
that love had disappeared.

but when i think of you baby
my mind says something different.
i'm just astonished by the opposing feeling
you give me.

talking to God about you

she might be the one and i'm excited about it.
God, i know that you see me and how i feel right now.
if she's the one then i've finally found her,
you finally gave the answer to my prayers.
she is too beautiful to describe in words from earth.
she is heavenly and that is all i can say,
and only you know what that truly means.
this woman has flaws of a diamond
that make no difference,
she is just as strong as one too.
i can't fathom my tongue in all the things she is to me,
my God, what have you done for me?
there is now no such thing i can strive for
that will make me happier on this planet.
my amazing God thank you,
she is all mine and we are both yours forever.
ugh, i think my heart loves her
and the rest of myself doesn't even know yet.

love in the garden

my partner in crime and repentance
let us be like adam and eve,
friends of God
and his most loved descendants.

love vs lust

your lust will die in battle against the sword
my search for love holds.
meaning the hunt you thirst for
is just pleasure in the moments that are gone
the next minute,
but my journey creates forces that cannot be
destroyed in all the moments that pass.
what i am looking for is not used by the eye but
with the mind,
so you will never be able to see this thing i am
talking about.
only in your head could you develop a picture
and see why it lasts longer
than the things you love with sight.

dear my love,

heaven

imagine you in the car with your partner,
but when you park in the driveway
you both exit from different doors
to get inside the house.
it's like this life with your spouse,
you are together for the ride
but when it's time to leave
you both have to go through your own door
that leads to your home.

if you love your partner,
care for that home,
and during the ride
ensure that you both know
how you'll be getting there.

my darling

i write to you my darling,
the eyes of the world see you more beautifully
than the precious stones of its core,
its butterflies surround your presence to enhance
their beauty and grace.
oh my darling the world regrets itself each night
that it has to stop shining its light on you,
the moon is ashamed to distract the sun from your
face at night,
it glows its moonlight as an apology.
to this earth you are its finest occupant,
oh but to me you are more than that.
to me you solidify that God hears my prayers,
my cries for a human that can share just a piece
of love that feels like His.
you are the answer and solution to my lonely heart,
a gift brought down to earth that God has also
given to me, i could never thank Him enough.
as for your delight in my eyes
they sparkle and widen in sight of you
and all of myself is opened
with a path in your direction.

dear my love,

i'll start by saying

my missing link to make this complete,
me, you, and Jesus are the strongest team.
i want us to show God what we can do,
that we can please him in the greatest way
and all we need to do is love His Son and each other,
we cannot ignore this opportunity.
how dare we miss this chance, i won't let it happen.
so take my hand now or i'll grab it myself
because we have something to do,
and i'll start by saying i love you.

back to light

right now i hope for smiles
and a cooling peace that relieves your tensions,
a crater that forms happiness in the moments you smile.
that is all i currently desire of you,
a meaningful stride towards God's beautiful plan for you.
other than this desire
it would bring me vast enchantment
to allow you the knowledge of the influence
you have on my life.
it is simple but far from faint,
but i admire your sweet gentleness
and strong love for Jesus Christ.
while you stay out of trouble
you still manage to lift His name on high.
it ignites feelings i have for you,
feelings of respect, applause, and truly deep admiration.
God Himself i'm sure favors you dearly.
i only ask that you remember to return to Him
after all dark misfortunes
just as day returns after every midnight hour.
in other words
keep being you relentlessly,
be the dawn and revert always back to light.

you love Him

i love you on earth with passion,
and if i love you like this
try to fathom and imagine how much
God loves you.
oh my baby,
my Lord and Savior weeps a million days
when your thoughts endure a sorrow
the world commits upon you.
but glory to His will that is highest,
glory to His plan for He still rewards those
who love Him,
and my darling you love Him.

paradise

this paradise you've welcomed me in
i would've never found
if you hadn't gone through the seas of sand and rock
to get here,
and still you appear so clean amongst the ground.
earth now knows its place in your life
for you are eternally strengthened,
forever flourished over the ground beneath you
just as the sun in the light of morning
so the dawn gives evil a warning.
you frighten wickedness.

.

after He created light

i feel almost unworthy to know it's touch
and the texture of your curves.
i look at my hands and think, what have they done
to deserve a trace of your waist?
should they ever know the sound of your skin
if my hands were down your back and my fingers
were to begin?
it doesn't feel right to have my ordinary wrists
that enable me to grip to ever grasp any part of you
that attracts my admiring eye.
and though i try not to lust at these areas of you
i occasionally forget,
but my mind stops before it claims a thought
that disrespects your modesty.
these things are true and if a day shall come that you
tell me your body is mine to hold,
my hands would never forgive me when it's time
to take them off your inviting frame.
finally, although your shape cannot be made any more
perfect and my eyes cannot be any more stuck in this
endless gaze,
you are a woman straight from eden
and a flower among the garden of perfection,
your body flourishes to capture God's wonderful work.

it's as though after He created light,
He thought of you
and waited to sculpt you until now.

God's will

it's hard to not fill with desire
amongst your presence,
it's such a persuasive beauty you carry
that seduces my being to want you.
i promise i fight it daily,
i do not want to intervene
because it is not my will,
but God's will be done
in the time he says.

purity

i refuse to accept my lustful feelings for you,
and although i can't deny that they exist
in my head,
out of respect for you i despise my involvement
in those thoughts.
my focus should be on your heart and only if
i should bring peace and happiness to your life.
but on nights like this, i think of things that are far
from occurring,
those far away days where my love goes past
hugs and kisses.
but enough of that, this has already gotten more
attention than deserved,
if possible forget all that i have mentioned
and know that i am focused on right now.
that incredible thing will be gifted to us later in life,
and the gift of being in love with you now continues
to grow.

she reminds me

such a great God you are,
while i don't even deserve your blessings
you still send me an angel from your golden land.
she helps me get closer to you
even in the sin i stand in.
sometimes i forget who my desire
should be bonded to,
and your angel reminds me that it is you
who gives and takes away,
and it is you who creates all beautiful things.
all from her toes and to her glamorous 5'3 frame,
just looking at her reminds me of all these things.

dear my love,

God's smile

do you think God is looking at us right now
and smiling?
the way we compliment each other, is it heavenly?
my darling, your smile would have the power
to bring forth rain upon a flower if it were up to me.
your happiness stays buried underneath my heart
that only breathes when you're the cause for it to beat.
it is a joy that i cherish in the most protected
parts of me.
a love like that can make the God of everything smile.

solomon

when we embrace each other
i strive to turn our two shadows into one,
to combine past human perception
under this vast and earthly sun.
that last line was used by a king
and just like him my soul of man
exists when i sing before God,
thanking Him for the dawn of my heart
which helps in battles against the world
and all odds.

doubts

it hurts me when you doubt yourself baby. i know in
the future you might face days where that consumes
your mind, and i promise there won't be an hour that
passes where i won't reassure you of your strength
and value. but i cannot tell a lie and say that it doesn't
sadden me when those doubts cover your lips, i even
wear this undesired anger that i war against. you don't
just doubt yourself, you doubt the woman i have
witnessed change my life and made it more beautiful.
you forget that you also doubt the woman i am so
deeply in love with. i am covered in joy by your love
and the way you are, i don't want you to change. i just
want you to be your real self, the you that isn't scared
to be fun and high spirited, the woman you were born
to be. i know that even God agrees with me on this,
and if He didn't, He wouldn't care to listen to all the
conversations i have about you with Him.
i love you my sunrise.

my equal

would you let me love you in the deepest way possible,
in an abyss that recognizes me and submits happily?
in this dimension let us allow endearment to be free
in depths of each other,
to explore endlessly and turn over all secrets?
let this be a chance to combine as one
fusing more than only the hearts of our souls.
be my equivalent so that God sees us as a single
form of His love.
we would be tied together by the strings of destiny,
ethereal gorgeousness would mold this attraction
and our Heavenly Father would accept its beauty,
for i know i am drawn to you in a way that is out of
my control– and i do not complain.
i know my being lives to die for your smile
and would die a second time for the chance to see
it twice.
i am not delusional or insane
but this thing we have is beyond even these words,
thankfully you know exactly what i mean.
my other part,
my heavenly half,
my equal.

dear my love,

i would mention you

our Heavenly Father and Eternal Savior,
the only one to overcome death who has no beginning
and no end.
our God who has power with no limit and love with no
condition, let's pursue Him first and we'll be alright.
like the rainbow He sent, rain won't drown this love.
my heart is yours but it is God's first and you love me
for that. beauty is vain, we know this to be true
but i'm talking about the beauty of God that lives inside
and all around you.
if He asked me face to face what do i have to say
about the one He had set aside for me, there would be
only a few things my mouth could utter
fighting to speak against His bright and powerful being.
in His presence i would fumble most of the strength
i have,
my eyes would stay closed to save me from going blind,
my mouth would barely open and my words
barely spoken,
but somehow with no air left i would plead a soft,
"thank you," and the chills in my spine would strengthen
for knowing that God heard my voice
in gratitude of you.

yes my love,
i would spend my irreplaceable time with Him
to mention you at least once
in His glorious presence.

at first sight

someone asked me
if i believed in love at first sight.
i told them i do,
i just don't know how often it happens.
i truly believe anything can happen,
nothing is exempt from existing
especially if you truly understand the power
of the one who created existence.

at first sight pt. two

He created you and i
and we fell in a love
that felt destined.
so i guess i don't know for sure
if it was at first sight,
but i do know that it happened
by God's orchestrated delight.

long distance

dear my love,

iceland

whenever i miss you
i sometimes look in the northeast direction
and i know in my heart that you are somewhere there
right in front of my eyes.
it's like i'm watching you be your normal beautiful self
even though i cannot actually see.
i guess you can say that i daydream.

i despise today

i miss you
and i can't do anything about it.
this has to be the worst thing
about love to exist.
my future with you is all i think about
because the present with you is absent
from my longing reality.

i love you already

God is teaching us patience.
this era that belongs only to us is torture,
it is a pain that i have to wait
to feel the kisses of your fingers on my skin.
it's not so much the absence of your hugs
that make me suffer,
but the embrace that our bodies will create
when we hold one another.
it's the sight of how your eyes lock onto every part
of my body,
you reveal yourself in that moment
for i see the desire on your face.
it's my passion that kills me to make a kind of love
to your lips in the moments of your gazes.
not only do i search to put your lips to mine
but it is also a pain to have to wait to say how i feel.
to be honest i'm in love with you
and i have been for a while,
i want to tell you now but God is making me wait
until i see you,
and though i agree with him,
my baby i love you right now
and i fight myself everyday
that you haven't heard me say it yet.

dear my love,

_____

_____

_____

_____

_____

_____

_____

_____

_____

_____

_____

anticipation

it's coming baby,
soon this dream will be yours.
gently coated kisses and tight grips
will cover you.
the countdown remains distant
but the truth is that it's close,
i can almost feel our love already.

soon to be

you are my garden of eden
my fruitful safe haven,
graceful daisies bloomed in your fragrance
enchant the passion in my voice.
i am lifted by your wind
and i fly by the gust of your soon to be kisses.
i cannot compare dust to a stone
just as a diamond cannot compare to your eyes.
like no other you remain separate from the world,
you are my soon to be lover
and my forever girl.

geography

what's weird is that my feelings are telling me
that in my ache for you
i grow too tired to even write,
to even think of a thought in the amount of you
that i miss.
but somehow, these words still found a piece of paper.
i am actually avoiding sleep so that i don't betray
you by not having your beautiful presence
in my thoughts.
even more so, i'm avoiding speaking on the phone
with you to keep a vow promised to my heart
that i would not add to its distress of being able
to hear your voice but not hold your body.
to hear words spoken from your captivating mind,
to see your face upon a screen
but not have the power or ability to send a kiss
to your cheek,
it is this geography that is tormenting me.

i wonder

will i still love you when i can't pull you close?
the absence of your sweet aroma,
will it remain in my head
while i stroll through the city of all these other smells
that are not yours?
your ethereal smile where there is no comparison for,
can i hold onto its image
without dying from my desire
of wanting you even more?

this way

i don't think it could've been done any other way.
i think it had to take some time to see your face,
for piles of paper to slowly turn into love letters.
it was meant to consist of facetime calls
and all night longs,
mornings with a head full of each others image
until the moment our voices became the signal
to start our day.
we were supposed to like each other
surviving on past texts of compliments
and flirtatious tension,
pictures and videos to replace our actual presence.
it was meant to be this way
so that right now,
we could be this way.

long distance

i can't wait until my mind and body
gets your touch again,
it'll be the best thing since you left me.

dear my love,

_____

_____

_____

_____

_____

_____

_____

_____

_____

_____

_____

note

i love the concept of letters, it forces the conversation to be heard until the end of a point. face-to-face, we are more likely to interrupt one's sentence, but in a letter you're forced to hear them through; before you interfere with your own thoughts you can think about theirs and analyze if you agree before you speak without consideration. you're able to listen and respond in love and understanding. it's a shame that's how regular conversations are supposed to be, it's just that most of us have lost our way.

dear my love,

just because flowers/2024

just because i want you to know that there's not a day in this new year that i won't love you entirely. i send these flowers to show that even though you're so far away i still ache to bring you romance, i also send this to show these flowers that the most beautiful thing to have grown on this earth is you. for they have never seen you before, but now they know. to you, the woman whom i keep falling in love with.

blind until then

i need the soft look of a gorgeous face
to put a smile on mine.
i am stuck in an era where a frown
is the only expression i know.
my skull feels heavy and it aches inside,
my eyelids cover half my eyes
and i see the world in a blur
through the spaces of my lashes.
too tired, too unmotivated to open them,
there is no use, no reason to fully see.
my vision has no meaning when there is nothing
beautiful to look at,
but if something breathtaking ever comes my way
through my unfocused eyes
it will sense delight
and automatically welcome its gorgeousness.
i will not need to force my pupils to see.
but until then,
until you,
i see no need.

my missing part

oh my sweet darling
how i wish i could caress you tightly
and feel the breath within your body.
that's how close i want you right now,
not miles away with an ocean between us.
my love, it hurts to feel this lonely,
i crave the graze of just a finger from your hands,
i need your aroma to surround my face
and enter the inner depths of me.
i would inhale like my nose was losing its smell
and remember it forever,
not a chance could i forget your scent
the way i yearn for you dearly.
how could i ever forget how i feel right now,
to be missing the part of me that is missing?

the sorrow i endure

my baby, my hurting remains starved
hungry for love that already belongs to me,
the love that you keep from me,
out of my reach in a land i have never been to.
untouched is my hands on your body in that
country my breath has not met.
unsafe is my heart without your love's protection.
it gets cold and you are my blankets,
i shiver in my bones until destruction
and my body aches in weakness.
i am exposed to all kinds of weather,
all kinds of pain.
i'm not sure if it is better to remain inside my
brokenness,
or act like it does not ache to have my greatest love
and deepest joy live each passing day without me.
my one and only, i have not known anyone
to know me like my beating heart does.

(continue next page)

i hear it cry to me about its bittersweet memory
you have tortured it with,
but it is clear that it is only torture because you have
been taken away
and it struggles to deal with your absence.
lastly i'll say again and just once more,
i cannot find the solution to this pain
so i ask that every now and then
when your sitting at home or waiting for the bus
that you remember that i am still working endlessly
to bring myself back to life so that i will have enough
strength to love you continuously,
to love you in that foreign nation with all of my heart
and all of my might.
and until then, i still love you.

trust me

don't be afraid to close your eyes
whether drowning in water or blinded in traffic,
i'm right here to give you sight in the darkness
you don't want to open your eyes in.
if we get through this wouldn't you then
believe me entirely?
then could there be no more issues of trust?
i'm hoping after this you would feel that you could
almost hand your heart over
and turn your head without a decimal of fear.
yes, i'm hoping you could look away
even with your heart in my hand.
if not, then we'll still be in the shadowy part of love,
we'll be scrambling for the faded reflections
of flickers to see.
i bet it is also cold in that region,
in this thing that i'm feeling.
i am saddened for i want your heart
with no strings on the end of it
because i would let you grab mine yourself,
but i sense trouble in your mental realm.
i can only ask you to please find anything
you can use to refuse what you have always
been doing.
deny what is easy and do it differently this time,
let distrust not find its breath,
let it choke on itself in darkness
and breathe in the light of your free mind.

dear my love,

a flight to england

i've always wanted to travel
and here i am on this turbulent shaken plane
fighting this fear and conquering my weaknesses
to chase after my heart's weakness.
i promise i feel this,
this strong and strange irreplaceable passion.
i'm laughing at your image in my imagination,
not of insults but of anxious happiness,
a racing feeling into your direction.
your beautiful complexion gives me issues
of impatience that cannot be solved until the time
of landing, until my worry can die and un-exist.
but this problem of waiting is worth the torture
for my reward is the beauty of a feeling
my heart anticipates for.
i can't wait to see you.

hopeless romance

worth it

it wasn't until i met you that time began to move
or the sun began to emit heat to the world
and to my skin.
life entered my life when you entered mine.
it sounds cliché
but the very known existence of your affection
towards me makes this world better,
at least in my eyes
the planet is now worth living for.

cannot be without

in my arms i held you so tenderly
but i was still firm.
it's like i was squeezing you tight,
holding you from someone trying to take you away.
it was weird realizing that my arms were not relaxed
but instead tense,
as if someone could pull you away from my grasp
if they wanted.
i either wanted to feel the weight of your entire
kind soul on my body,
or i was scared, and hypothetically
delusionally preventing you from abduction.
now knowing the taste of your love,
i cannot lose you over anything.

familiar face

i just don't know if i'm going to find you.
what if you don't even exist?
what if i made you up
too unrealistic?
what if we meet and i don't recognize your face?
is it possible for one to lose their soulmate
just for someone else to wander the world with them
in your place?
i feel like it is and that scares me,
i intensely hope i am not so stupid
that i see a stranger upon your face.

thankfully, none of this was true
because i knew exactly who you were
when i met you.

universe of reasons

i have a universe full of reasons why we
should fall in love.
there are storms that form deserts
with grains of sand that count the same number
of times i would call you beautiful.
hands with creases and folds that would build
homes for you,
planets of dirt and rock that hold it in place
to rest your temple.
there are seas of galaxies full of tears
that i would cry to ensure that if you want a ship,
it would float.
cold depths and echoes of chaos
that i would burn to bring you warmth,
and darkness that i would rob
so that you could see.
these are all but only a thought of reasons
i'm talking about.

there is still the rest of a universe of reasons
why we should fall in love.

disguise

i would promise to wear a disguise
if it were to protect your heart.
love is scary
and i know that i would always put you first
even if it means wearing some kind of mask
to take away the risk of hurting you.
but still you would recognize my devotion
and see right through me,
as if i could somehow hide
how much i am in love with you.

you could:

love me while i love you
embrace me while i love you
hurt me while i love you
ignore me while i love you
forget me while i love you
either way, i still want you.

dear my love,

my stranger

sail away with me
and as much salt is in this sea
think of my heart with so much love in me.
if you could taste my heart
there would be too much salt on your tongue
to pretend it's not there.
be my partner or be my sailor
but if you say no,
if you are anything to me at all,
at least be my stranger.
in that way somehow,
someway,
you'll still be mine.

romeo and juliet

let me die in the name
of what i've been chasing,
and if i shall stay down
then let it be love
that made it okay.

better to have loved and lost

i would love for someone to urge me in the direction
of the possibility of great heartache
for that is the only way i will know i have found someone
i am sincerely fond of.
who would i be to rather a kind of love that does not
care if we have no deep desire for each other,
no impatience of time when we are apart;
over a love that hurts like the death of existence
when i lose their touch?
i am smart enough to have no interest in things
that bring me vacant and meaningless moments,
feelings that do not classify as emotion.
i would much rather experience feelings of sorrow
from the greatest loss of love my heart could possess
than to have a heart that never truly felt alive
in all of its millions of heartbeats.

life before you

this lonely itch
still lives beside me.
when i lay down
when i drive at night
when i wake up in the morning.
at any moment that itch
comes to boast that i have no one,
that i need someone,
even if just for a second,
and i scratch it every time.

you already have

love is born
when hearts are found in the same place.
too often they pass by one another
and rarely do they stop and notice
that they have found each other.
all it takes is a second,
but the time of a heart moves quickly.
a day is an hour,
a second is half of a moment
and still so many of us are impatient.

when will someone notice mine?

is it too much?

i want to be a prize like you.
i perfectly desire you know that your value to me
is much higher than my own,
but still i want to be a special something
that you would regret if you ever lost,
i want to be irreplaceable.
you are more than all precious metals and jewels,
the apple of my eye and my highest honor,
my walking miracle,
but is it possible that i be priceless too?
is it too much to ask that just like you
i be recognized as a prize you could ever mourn?
could you admit that if you were to lose me,
my incomparable love would cause you pain
as well?

then you came

i deserve the love i give to others.
well i think,
i mean i bend my back to give,
should i not be given anything in return?
should i not be shown appreciation
in the currency i lack?
for humanity's sake i hope my supply never runs out.
what would we do if my love was wasted
until there was none left?
a question i have no control over
because it seems
like there is no one else left on earth
who wants to hold it carefully.

my ending

if i ever lost what treasure i have found
floating away from the shoreline,
should there ever be a day
you are anywhere else but here,
the air could not save me
from my own loss of breath.
pain would be the execution of my brain
and the extinction of joy would end me.

first and last

you are my first true love and i hope my last,
it hurts to think that one day
you could be my first, but also my past.
i wouldn't know what to say
i wouldn't know what i'd do
it just might kill the very half of me
that is also all of you.

this book

i'm so in love that i wrote a book of poetry
with words of *ink* using the blood of love
to describe how you make me feel
and how i feel for you.
this entire collection is already tattooed
into the deeper layers of myself.
the *pages* are like the stages of which it grew,
the *letters* are the seconds i spent with you.
i've told myself, these are the moments
i never want to forget.
the *cover* is the front of my heart
sheltering this place that you are held,
the *pictures* only display a portion
of the true affliction i have
when you're away from me.
most of this was written apart from you,
so you can imagine how lonely it is
when i spend my days remembering you.
the *reader* is like the world applauding
your elegant effect on me
for i take delight in the eyes of thousands
knowing i have fallen deeply for you.
this book is simply another effort to express
my unchanging feelings.
to you, my dear love.

you don't have to say it back

i love you and you don't have to say it back,
shall my ears not hear
or feel the sound of those words back
press no regret in the air in which words
were already spoken,
my breath still serves as the owner of this verse.
i don't need to know if you love me back,
i just need you to know that i am in love with you.

while you sleep

when you hung up and went to sleep
so did i,
only i actually stayed awake thinking of you
unable to rest my eyes,
not ready to die,
not without a little more of you.
i couldn't believe i found myself up at 12:42 AM
fighting my sleep to quench this despair.
i imagined times in the future
grinning at moments i wished for.
i resided in endless joy at your smile in these
visions and dreams,
i do not regret your sleep for beauty needs rest,
i am just selfish at times
and i want you awake for my own sake.
i hope you understand my coping mechanism
and why tomorrow i might still be tired.
it's because at times when you don't need me
i still need you,
at least to help me not need you for a little while.
i am eager for that morning hour
but for now i'll talk to you tomorrow,
at dawn.

reading "while you sleep" to you

tears started to form in your eyes
but you wouldn't allow them to fall,
not in front of me– not yet at least.
knowing i touched a part of your heart
that made you cry solidified my never ending
desire to write for you infinitely.
not to force tears of sorrow
but to birth raindrops from heaven,
the land of peace and love from your eyes
down to the bottom of your chin.

may 18th, 2024

i just want you to know that i'm trying my best to be the best for myself, and to give you the kind of love you deserve, especially since you're so far away. baby, i am at a constant effort in my mind to have a future with you, and not just any future, but one worthy of you. you are a child straight from God, you are the kindest and most caring person i ever met, and when i look at you i see someone that should be cared for and loved in the same way that you do for others. it's not fair that you have been mistreated all this time in the past, and i just want to remind you that you are wonderful and impressively beautiful, not just your face but everything. the butterflies in my heart break out of their cocoons because of the unbearable joy i get from loving you. i can't explain it any more visually accurate but, you're the spark in my mind like a creative idea. i'm in love with you so much and i sometimes destroy myself because of thoughts of you accidentally forgetting that truth. but still, nothing would change if you ever did forget, i would simply pour my heart out as if it were my first time falling for you again. heartbreak from you would be eleven times worse than any other form of brokenness. the good thing is that the complete solution and cure to that ache, is simply a single most faultless smile occurring from your heart mending complexion. ultimately, i'm in love with my undying calling to put this feeling to work, just so that i can enter a cycle that discovers happiness at the mere sight of you.

date: _____

_____

_____

_____

_____

_____

_____

_____

_____

_____

_____

_____

_____

_____

i hate

i hate the way fire doesn't warm me
like it does when you're near.
i still feel a coldness resisting its comfort.
it's just like when my smile resists its curve
when you're not here.
but when you are
i find myself smiling for no reason at all.

i hate

_____

_____

_____

_____

_____

_____

_____

_____

_____

_____

_____

however dark it gets

even the empty seat in which you once sat
brings me sadness.
my lap that you once rested your head upon
bombards my mind with past tense.
i miss the way i felt when you made me smile,
white flowers and the early sun brings a picture
of you to my eyes,
it reminds me that between you and i
is still a while.
i dig up piles of nothings in wait of you,
so many files of unhappy stories fill my shelves.
i long for the days i get to see you tomorrow,
for those come only a few every season
and my being without you is a darkness
that even in the light you cannot see.
i miss you,
and darling i will wait regardless
of how dark it gets.

dear my love,

is it?

i can only love you with happily bloomed tulips
and roses,
soft mornings and delicate words
lifting your soul to a happy place,
cool nights with deep conversations
invading your heart
to better know how to protect it.

i can only love you in colors,
in vibrant hues and pastels
in crayons and acrylic paint;
art submits to you
and fathoms a true masterpiece.

i can only love you in peace,
in silence and in noise
your ear caresses its drum,
a soothing tenderness remains.

i can only love you like these things,

is it enough?

dear my love,

forever my baby

if we ever broke up
and lost the path we were walking on,
someday in time if we were to meet again
the name i would use to call your face
to my direction would still be "baby."
broken up and separated
you are still my baby.
even if you reject that title,
even if my love has no more meaning to you,
my mouth would still only know you as baby.
i wouldn't be able to apologize if you became
disgusted, because you are mine
unconditionally,
and the fact of you and i not being together
doesn't change the fate of who you are
to my eternal heart.

passion & intimacy

dear my love,

even more

in the dark your voice lightens the mood
i see your soul when it talks to me,
every word brings it closer to mine
almost touching our souls combine,
invested and secure
let's entangle even more.

rude

i've grown unable
to resist your lips,
looking at you speak
and wanting to interrupt.
please forgive my rudeness
if you don't finish your sentence.

unnameable

what will you name it when our kisses
melt onto each other's lips?
when our tongues hold the taste
of generous passion?
what will you call this unity of sweet fire
if a kiss is not enough to describe it?
what if you forget to breathe
and you come up like you were drowning in ecstasy?
would that intimacy intimidate you
to keep a few of your walls up?

i would rather not touch at all
than to have you miss the entirety of my passion.
just this once, so i know that you know the feeling,
forget that air exists,
forget how to draw breath into your lungs
and just kiss me like you want to fall in love.

mind

my ways tie together with yours
and these thoughts morph into a bind
that is trapped upon a bond unable to be shaken.
my mind is mistaken with days of it not receiving
you from my eyes,
but i am still relieved because i find memories
that tie you back in.
this way i am never separate from the other mind
mine so obsessively needs.

touch

i've been a servant to this touch,
there's no artist that could sculpt a better version
of your skin; just my luck.
but after some thought
i then embrace this situation
because i only groan about the time i don't
get to have you,
when the distance becomes real again.
i am a happy slave
to the soft and sound touch of your skin,
but for now you are mine.

you can be indecisive about things

your every want if you speak it to my ear
will be done with urgency.
your changing mind and indecisive mouth
matter to me none.
my pursuit changes at the breath of your voice
in just the lift of your tongue.
it is your love that i work for,
from the sound your beautiful mind makes
to its so many different dreamy aspirations.

heart

my heart is full,
drenched by a harmless fire
and a heavy passion.
it is scarred with a mark
that cannot be healed,
forever tainted.
though this thing is sweet
and never skewed
this scar is warm and precious,
my heart is convicted
with unchanging action
and it fully takes responsibility.
my heart is bound by a love
it has no explanation for,
it is found guilty
and eager to serve its sentence.

i dare you

my darling i dare you to try not to recognize
yourself inside of me,
i am confident that you will see the influence
you have.
every freckle and spot on my body knows you by name
and turns into stars in your presence.
my hands imitate the vessels on your heart
for they are proud to show off who they belong to.
darling, if you look at me it is purely impossible
to not see a little bit of you.

thirsty for you

my mouth is dry
and i thirst for water
in the same breath
i crave a drink of you.
my yearn is parched
and your attention is refreshing,
it replenishes my body.
like this water i drink
you are essential
for my well being,
and now i'm thirsty again,
but not for water.

dear my love,

sweet like honey

you are so sweet my gentle lover.
have you bathed in honey,
my aphrodite?
have you given approval
for it to sink into your skin
to allow your soul to taste like honey?
it will attract me for my entire life,
till my days grow old.
though this taste also rejuvenates,
i am vigorously lost in this world of you
and your great kindness.
my queen, my lovely lady,
you are sweet and incredibly fine
i am fond in a way too strong
to call love,
the nectar you speak is too sweet
for the bees to drink up,
but for me, my heart's tongue is complete
after a taste of you.
you are so sweet,
and honey,
you are all mine.

moment

slowly
so closely
right in front of me,
pretend we have no mind
solely existing
with no conscience
stored inside.

slow

dance with me
for we speak love in many languages,
though this one is absent from our lives.
could we encapsulate this romance and pause
to read our souls in each other's eyes?
my darling, let's slow down,
allow me to spin you around
and embrace my guiding hands.
paint this air with your presence among myself,
let this music become the canvas we dance upon,
twist and tangle my heart with yours,
and let's appreciate the slowness of love
in this very moment.

a lonely night with you

i just want one night
trapped inside a box of windows
in a room filled with once in a lifetimes,
a fireplace and dark skies outside of you and i.
i want us to feel something invisible,
something that cannot be held.
i can't help but die for this imagination of us,
feeling this moment that lasts all night
but also our whole lives.
it's not an act, but the feeling of our souls
getting stuck to each other's that i crave.
it would be our deepest memory creating itself,
the nerves in my body would tingle and vibrate
in this moment,
and so it captures my gut feeling
and all of these butterflies in my stomach
like a picture.

for us only

i want us to have private access to each other,
access that only i can unlock
and only you can view.
this exclusiveness is attractive
and i say let's continue in this respectable
seduction of each other.

pure love

core memory

the world in the lens of a child
carries senses that are higher than adults.
their experiences are so much more intense,
their memories are engrained
much more permanently.
love me like a child loves,
like a core memory.

my piece of happiness

i have a woman
gorgeous and kind
she is especially beautiful
and incredibly fine,
my love you are fire
and my fingers
is the hand uncontrolled.
you are a diamond
and my heart is the ring
that tries to be gold.
my darling, you are the love
my soul longs to hold,
through every moment of laughter
your simple presence
is the best piece of happiness
i will ever chase after.

dear my love,

believers

some people can't believe
what they haven't seen,
so they won't believe
that this kind of love exists
until we walk in it.

let's make them believers

the vow

out in the garden
where we planted the seeds
we dug and got deep.
we hit where the root would be
and replaced that emptiness with a seed.
we covered it to hold it in place,
we watered it because we knew what could grow.
during harvest season
we got exactly what we expected.

what was the seed you might ask?
the seed was a vow to work through the ground;
to give an effort to understand each other.
the seed was merely an opportunity
for something beautiful to grow.

i searched and i have found

they ask what i love?
i say preciousness.

i look for naturalness,
created epitomes of heaven,
unique souls in ordinary bodies,
the kind that assumes the attraction of everything.
i look for invisible intentions of purity
that can shrink evils to dust.
my vision becomes consumed with its grace
and grows in its direction.
transformed and blossomed
i am renewed and loved by all that is good.
this is why i have been looking for you.

her

all is within her
in the veins of her capacity
stretched through her skin of golden simplicity.
realms of her mind compelled to explore
and discover.
she invites love because she is made of it.
fierce and steady, she struggles but fights,
passion, hunger, and absolutely with light.

the sun loves poetry

i woke up before the dawn
and could not go back to sleep
before writing you into the universe,
i couldn't bear the guilt
of leaving you out of the world.
so there in my bed i wrote,
i wrote until the sun fell in love with you.
he read my poems and understood
why i couldn't go to sleep.

stuck

to the one whom i cannot unravel from,
when we first met
i uncovered the truth that no woman
can be crafted anymore beautifully than you.
and now i still wake up in my bed
with that exact same thought.
i suppose my heart is eternally stuck in time
in love with you.

your affection

it is strange to realize
that everyone else's affection
has no effect like yours.
it is different in ways i do not understand,
but i am still compelled to find out
why my body feels like it has entered
a space in heaven when you hold me.

new kind

i fell in love
and it has been like nothing
i've ever felt before.
that is until today where it suddenly feels
like i am just now discovering this.

the truth is that
i have actually just fallen deeper in love,
it is a whole new kind
that has now left the older one behind.

and i feel like a lot of people say this
without actually feeling the effects of it,
the reality of the increase.

baby, i genuinely fall more in love with you
every time God blesses us with the opportunity
to see each other. We have never done long
distance before so all of this is still a new thing you
and i are experiencing, but quite literally i have
never loved you as much as i do now. i love you all
the way from california to england.

if you were a painter

i'd ask you to paint me.
a singer?
i'd ask you to sing to me.
if you were to look at me
i'd just ask that you kiss me.
moral of the story
is that for everything that you are,
there is also a request i have
to experience more of you.

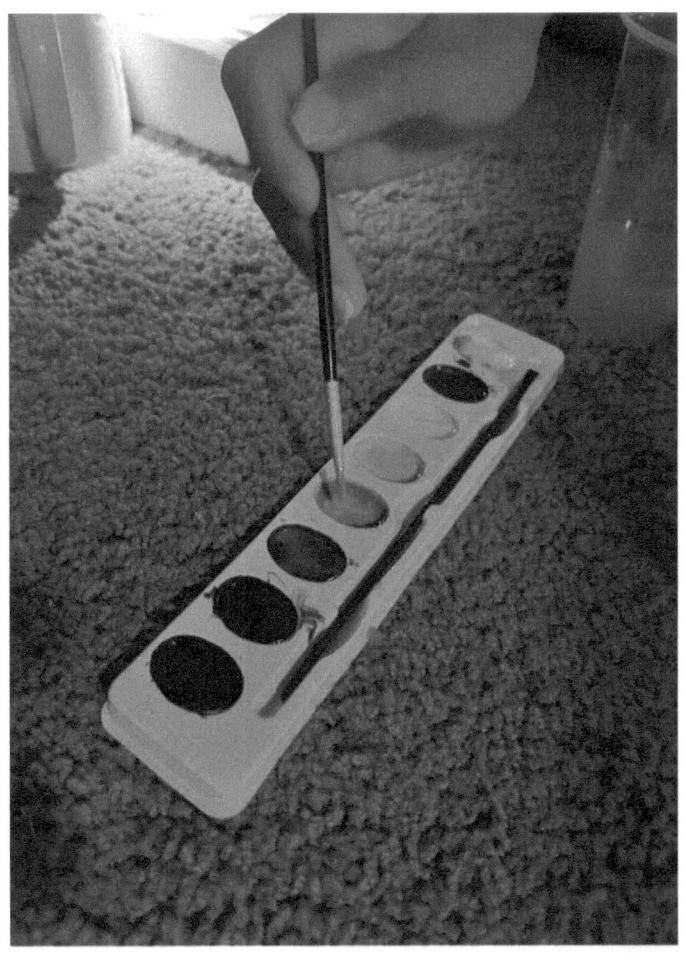

forever young

like kids just for tonight
let's go under the covers
with little to no air to breathe
and whisper "i love you's,"
and maybe a flashlight
to tell stories we have yet to share.
if we just pretend,
i feel young love will unveil itself
like we had it all along.

only if

what does it mean to lead with love?
if i shall bleed
from fighting battles to keep you safe
would that finally be enough?
if i save your village and declare that they are free,
would love mean to you
what it has always meant to me?
when i leave pride and greed to follow far behind,
will you grab my hand as we go into this land
i dream of taking you?
so yes, i will lead with love,
but only if you follow me into it.

dear my love,

_____

_____

_____

_____

_____

_____

_____

_____

_____

_____

_____

my pleasure

i've seen you cry too many times
to be the reason tears fall
from the most precious face of all.
i pledge myself to bear the sorrows directed at you.
let my face drown from my eye
so that yours remains dry,
let my own heart break
so that you become the cause for joy
when my smile is restored from frowning,
and when my face is saved from drowning.
it would be my pleasure.

dear my love,

written by her

losing sleep thinking about your kind brown eyes.
losing patience thinking about when i will be fortunate
enough to be in your arms.
losing my ability to track time when talking to you.
losing my memory of people that have done me wrong
to make space for memories with you.

these are the things i'm willing to lose to gain a YOU.

love never fails

thunder and lightning
it's loud and bright,
it's dim and silent
under orders of the sky.

a wonder but frightening
with power it strikes,
here and there
but never here twice.

thunder and lightning
in a heart when it likes,
now and forever
because when it starts
it won't die.

secret spot

i want a secret spot with you,
a place we go to be alone
with no distractions.
a place where only our hearts make sounds.
i want to find a spot where when we meet,
we know love waits for us
and anger is not allowed.
in this spot anger must be forgotten.
so let this be an unspoken agreement
to allow our love to rule.

dilated

your words bring light to my dark eyes.
my pupil's emptiness grows outside of itself
and it accepts the light you shine.
your words remain encased inside forever
remembering peace in my darkness
and light when you speak to me.

a feeling with no name

the hair on my arms rose up,
a sense ignited my fire.
gutted in my stomach,
a feeling with a sharp corner,
a decision and desire.
i wrestle enemies
to reveal this thing
until my hairs can go no higher.

soul over shape

we all focus on the strengthening of our bodies
and the pleasantness of our shape
while the integrity of our hearts are weak
and unhealthy.
it means nothing to perfect our physique
when it withers to dust after a hundred years.
but the kindness of our soul endures forever
due to the love we have for its life.
i challenge everyone to search and see
if the exercise you do for your attractive body
matches the food you give
to nourish your valuable soul.

i'm blessed to know that your incredible body equals
your incredible soul

less is more

honestly i try to find different ways to say this,
in one way i say, "all the stars suspended in space
don't amount to the one you have placed in my heart."
or i say,
"my traveling spirit that lives only to chase after you
longs for its destination."

these sayings still
for reasons i cannot understand,
do not sufficiently replace a simple set of words.
three words, that unfortunately is said commonly
in vein,
but in its truthfulness
when from a voice of delicate emotion,
from a mouth to an ear
and the space in the air that carries its sound,
these words that reveal themselves as surely
impassioned are,

"i love you."

i don't want to

i wish i could forget you
but your kisses sung a melody
my head remembered after only hearing once.
your scent stung like a bee
that wanted to inject peace instead of pain,
i melted away from chills of spiced fragrance.
i wish i could forget you
but the truth is that i don't ever want to.

stranded in paris

cold and numb
stiff and toes that ached
legs that walked too long past the night's moon.

we had a whole world to ourselves,
the silence of the city
with only the noise of our adventures
to make a sound.
lights that kept the streets perfect
for walking and talking,
yes it was ice cold and barely bearable
but i still want to get stranded in paris with you.

again.

dear my love,

too huge

she asked if i had a poem to cheer her up?
she said she was feeling small and low,
so i put my cape on as this moment needed a hero.
i thought, how could she feel so low
when i see her in the sky every morning,
amidst the clouds in the orange and pink light
carrying her wonder to the land i walk on?
how could she think she is small
when the amount she has bloomed into my heart
is bigger than my body?
these feelings from her don't even fit,
they are too huge for me to carry all at once.
i have spend long days just empty myself
of all this poetry,
and still, my hand cannot stop writing of her.

terrarium

her heart was pacing
and mine was racing.
she couldn't settle on decisions
and i couldn't keep my cool around her.
we seemed like two knuckleheads
in need of a partner with structure,
someone of order and not each other.
whether that's true or not
doesn't destroy the fact that we still somehow work.
joy rains down every evening
despite our early troubles.
who would we be to turn down
such a sustaining system of love?

dear my love,

_____

_____

_____

_____

_____

_____

_____

_____

_____

_____

_____

_____

can i do these for you?

you talk to me with respect
and i'm treated like royalty catered by your voice.
you devote goodness to me because of the nurturing
gift God has designed into you.
you are touched with gold and the aroma of heaven.
though my heart has been in the sand for some time
you picked it up and saw treasure,
a treasure i assumed no one was looking for.
you designate an island for me
where i reside all day long.
in your head, we live lifetimes in love together.
i stumble in my mouth like my words lost balance,
i try to speak against your doe eyes,
both moments i become weak and strong in.
those eyes hold a power that inspire me for the better,
and at the same time your eyes cause me an
irresistible tongue,
i also cannot resist saying yes to every one of your
requests.
you make me never regret giving part of my life to you.
every facetime sleepover,
all the jaw dropping and mouth drooling pictures you
send me,
every super cheesy smile you try to hide from me,
all the prayers i know you pray for me,
all the thoughts of love and safety you think over me.

all of these things you do for me,
i just ask,
would you please let me do these for you?

dear my love,

_____

_____

_____

_____

_____

_____

_____

_____

_____

_____

_____

love is invisible

love is not something you can physically feel like
getting hit in the chest, although it sometimes feels
like that. it is an invisible feeling, born in a thought
that either grows stronger or never exists. it does not
reside in the human body, but in the spirit of a soul.
as the world progresses, we realize how hard it is for
people to believe in things they cannot see, this
explains why there are so many of us who are living
without a heart. if love was something you could
capture in a picture then earth would be more
peaceful, but that is not the case. it cannot be
tangibly proven, therefore not many understand it.
to understand love, you first need to accept the
presence of things you cannot see. because of this,
love is spiritual and cannot be seen in the same way
our eyes can see an object. our bodies do not hold
any ounce of it within its skin, but it is inside the
invisible parts of us. that is where we hold this thing
called love. so, it is either created in the soul and
cemented by a Heavenly Designer, or it isn't real at
all, and you must admit that even something known
to be as sacred as love is just a figment of your
imagination and holds no real meaning or purpose.
so again i say, you either become enslaved to the
limited knowledge of humanity by only using your
mortal body to understand and believe; or you use
your heart, soul, and spirit to understand the reality
of the world and the things unseen that are still
found within us.

do you believe in love even though you cannot hold it?
if yes, then i wonder who or what else you can believe
in without visual proof.

a lion's pride

you may be proud of your crown,
proud to be a king of great gold and pride
and to let diamonds shine glory above your head,
but my throne is not a seat of wealth and power.
sure, i am no king without a crown of my own
but mine is not one with treasures of gold
and jewels that compliment my hair,
the very crown that makes me king
is my glorious queen.

she makes my empire a kingdom of greatness
and love.
if she leaves me alone then i simply become a man
in a chair with a hat on his head,
a lion with a mane with just some hair that i'll shed,
but with her
i lead against mountains of evil and hyenas.
like a lion with a humble province,
i protect and love,
i remain gentle and strong towards my pride
so that we remain thankful and empowered
by our Father up above.

dear my love,

stain

i love you so beautifully
it stains dark rooms with light.
my teeth reeks of laughter.
sheets and pillows,
the clothes on my body
marked by you and your
fantastic aroma,
it all seeps so far
and too deep to get out.
my life is beautifully stained by you
and i cannot get you out.

the prettiest flower

this dirt path i wander on
in the eyes of dandelions
and lupine families,
i encounter their peace
and the sun and wind
completes their happiness.
there is also a bush of delight,
bright red and healthy green stems.
i gaze into the heart of roses and listen
to the beauty they call themselves.
"such a majestic piece of life," they sing,
"the prettiest of all the flowers," i hear them say.
i smile as they go on
and i respond with smug,

"you don't know my Dawn."

in case you noticed the frequent use of the word *dawn* throughout this book, it is because that is the name of my dear love, **Dawn.**

yours only,

ariel

About the Author

Ariel West Jr is a young black and latino poet with a natural interest for how words are arranged. Author of *Daydream, the need of light and you*, and *dear my love*, has a great love for the outdoors and is probably somewhere fishing if he is nowhere else to be found. He is actively growing in his art as a writer and plans to write forever. You can follow and connect with him on Instagram @arielwestjr. Post and tag him in your favorite pages or to show off the amazing book cover!

Dedicate a poem to a loved one or the entire book!

"The purpose of this book is to inspire others to love. This is the same for all my books, but this one is special. This book I hope to inspire people to wait on a love that is beautiful and fulfilling, a kind that is different from how the world says love is found and experienced. I hope that this book shows you that a relationship that God approves of, is worth waiting for. God is the Creator of love, and only He knows who can bind your heart into a love you will never find without Him. He has someone who is kind, respectful, patient, forgiving, and willing to love you regardless of your faults. And if not, He has someone who is willing to try every single day to be that for you, that is the love He has for us. Dawn, I thank Jesus for you, and I hope you see this book as just a fraction of how gratefully in love I am with you." -ariel west jr

I give all the glory to God because he gave me the insight and motivation to create this art about what he says is the most important thing for us to do. Love.

index

Cover art created by Josephine West.

Pictures taken and legally owned by Ariel West Jr.

www.arielwestjrpoetry.com

ISBN: 979-8-218-54576-5